THE AMARA WOMAN WELLNESS JOURNAL

THE AMARA WOMAN WELLNESS JOURNAL

DR. YVETTE MAUREEN

Copyright © 2021 Dr. Yvette Maureen

All rights reserved. No part of this book may be reproduced, stored, or transmitted by any means—whether auditory, graphic, mechanical, or electronic—without written permission of both publisher and author, except in the case of brief excerpts used in critical articles and reviews. Unauthorized reproduction of any part of this work is illegal and is punishable by law.

Because of the dynamic nature of the Internet, any web addresses or links contained in this book may have changed since publication and may no longer be valid. The views expressed in this work are solely those of the author and do not necessarily reflect the views of the publisher, and the publisher hereby disclaims any responsibility for them.

INTRODUCTION

The AMARA Woman Wellness Journal is a compilation of weekly thought-provoking and soul-searching exercises. Each week provides an emotional and nutrition check point to help readers gauge their progress in meeting fitness and general goals.

'Motivation Central' asks readers to reflect on their weekly inspiration while affirming the next positive step to take after working out.

'Gratitude Moment' provides readers an opportunity to express feelings of gratitude and appreciation each week.

Inspirational and instructional quotes are integrated within the weekly journal pages so that readers may respond to their most intimate thoughts or write their thoughts related to each theme.

This journal integrates all the dimensions of wellness—balancing emotional, social, and spiritual health for total well-being and self-responsibility.

DATE _____ / _____ / _____

GOALS FOR THE WEEK

☐ A fitness goal for the week is: _____
_____

☐ A general goal for the week is: _____
_____

MOTIVATION CENTRAL

This week, I feel inspired by: _____

After working out, I'm totally going to: _____
_____

HOW AM I DOING?

Emotional Check-In

All in all, this week was:
_____
_____

One thing I think I did well this week:
_____
_____

Nutrition Check-In

The good and bad of my food this week:
_____
_____

Days that I drank 8 glasses of water:

[S] [M] [T] [W] [T] [F] [S]

GRATITUDE MOMENT

This week, I feel thankful for: _____
_____
_____
_____

COMPLIMENT SOMEONE EVERY DAY.

_____
_____
_____
_____
_____
_____
_____
_____
_____
_____

SAY "THANK YOU" AND "PLEASE" A LOT.

_____
_____
_____
_____
_____
_____
_____
_____
_____
_____

DATE ____ / ____ / _____

GOALS FOR THE WEEK

☐ A fitness goal for the week is: _____
_____

☐ A general goal for the week is: _____
_____

MOTIVATION CENTRAL

This week, I feel inspired by: _____

After working out, I'm totally going to: _____
_____

HOW AM I DOING?

Emotional Check-In

All in all, this week was:
_____
_____

One thing I think I did well this week:
_____
_____

Nutrition Check-In

The good and bad of my food this week:
_____
_____

Days that I drank 8 glasses of water:

[S] [M] [T] [W] [T] [F] [S]

GRATITUDE MOMENT

This week, I feel thankful for: _____
_____
_____
_____

THE AMARA WOMAN WELLNESS JOURNAL | 7

HAVE A PURE HEART AND A BALANCED LIFE.

DO NOT BE AFRAID TO ADMIT WHEN YOU'RE WRONG.

DATE ____/____/_____

GOALS FOR THE WEEK

☐ A fitness goal for the week is: _____
_____

☐ A general goal for the week is: _____
_____

MOTIVATION CENTRAL

This week, I feel inspired by: _____

After working out, I'm totally going to: _____
_____

HOW AM I DOING?

Emotional Check-In

All in all, this week was:
_____
_____

One thing I think I did well this week:
_____
_____

Nutrition Check-In

The good and bad of my food this week:
_____
_____

Days that I drank 8 glasses of water:

[S] [M] [T] [W] [T] [F] [S]

GRATITUDE MOMENT

This week, I feel thankful for: _____
_____
_____
_____

USE YOUR POWER TO STOP WHAT IS NO LONGER GOOD FOR YOU.

_____
_____
_____
_____
_____
_____
_____
_____
_____

HONOR YOUR FEELINGS NO MATTER WHAT THEY ARE.

_____
_____
_____
_____
_____
_____
_____
_____
_____

DATE ____ / ____ / _____

GOALS FOR THE WEEK

☐ A fitness goal for the week is: _____
_____

☐ A general goal for the week is: _____
_____

MOTIVATION CENTRAL

This week, I feel inspired by: _____

After working out, I'm totally going to: _____
_____

HOW AM I DOING?

Emotional Check-In

All in all, this week was:
_____
_____

One thing I think I did well this week:
_____
_____

Nutrition Check-In

The good and bad of my food this week:
_____
_____

Days that I drank 8 glasses of water:

[S] [M] [T] [W] [T] [F] [S]

GRATITUDE MOMENT

This week, I feel thankful for: _____
_____
_____
_____

THE AMARA WOMAN WELLNESS JOURNAL | 15

BE THE FIRST TO SAY 'HELLO'.

___

ACKNOWLEDGE, ACCEPT, AND EMBRACE EVERYTHING ABOUT YOU.

___

DATE ____ / ____ / _____

GOALS FOR THE WEEK

☐ A fitness goal for the week is: _____
_____

☐ A general goal for the week is: _____
_____

MOTIVATION CENTRAL

This week, I feel inspired by: _____

After working out, I'm totally going to: _____
_____

HOW AM I DOING?

Emotional Check-In

All in all, this week was:
_____
_____

One thing I think I did well this week:
_____

Nutrition Check-In

The good and bad of my food this week:
_____
_____

Days that I drank 8 glasses of water:

[S] [M] [T] [W] [T] [F] [S]

GRATITUDE MOMENT

This week, I feel thankful for: _____
_____
_____
_____

WHAT OTHER PEOPLE THINK ABOUT YOU IS NOT YOUR CONCERN.

_____

_____

_____

_____

_____

_____

_____

_____

LIVE BENEATH YOUR MEANS.

_____

_____

_____

_____

_____

_____

_____

_____

DATE ____ / ____ / _____

GOALS FOR THE WEEK

☐ A fitness goal for the week is: _____
_____

☐ A general goal for the week is: _____
_____

MOTIVATION CENTRAL

This week, I feel inspired by: _____

After working out, I'm totally going to: _____
_____

HOW AM I DOING?

Emotional Check-In

All in all, this week was:
_____
_____

One thing I think I did well this week:
_____
_____

Nutrition Check-In

The good and bad of my food this week:
_____
_____

Days that I drank 8 glasses of water:

[S] [M] [T] [W] [T] [F] [S]

GRATITUDE MOMENT

This week, I feel thankful for: _____
_____
_____
_____

THE AMARA WOMAN WELLNESS JOURNAL | 23

BE FORGIVING OF YOURSELF AND OTHERS.

TAKE THE TIME TO DEVELOP YOUR MIND.

DATE _____ / _____ / _____

GOALS FOR THE WEEK

☐ A fitness goal for the week is: _____
_____

☐ A general goal for the week is: _____
_____

MOTIVATION CENTRAL

This week, I feel inspired by: _____

After working out, I'm totally going to: _____
_____

HOW AM I DOING?

Emotional Check-In

All in all, this week was:
_____
_____

One thing I think I did well this week:
_____
_____

Nutrition Check-In

The good and bad of my food this week:
_____
_____

Days that I drank 8 glasses of water:

[S] [M] [T] [W] [T] [F] [S]

GRATITUDE MOMENT

This week, I feel thankful for: _____
_____
_____
_____

THE AMARA WOMAN WELLNESS JOURNAL | 27

BE CONFIDENT THAT YOU POSSESS ALL YOU NEED TO SUCCEED.

MAKE NEW FRIENDS BUT CHERISH THE OLD ONES.

DATE _____ / _____ / _____

GOALS FOR THE WEEK

☐ A fitness goal for the week is: _____
_____

☐ A general goal for the week is: _____
_____

MOTIVATION CENTRAL

This week, I feel inspired by: _____

After working out, I'm totally going to: _____
_____

HOW AM I DOING?

Emotional Check-In

All in all, this week was:
_____
_____

One thing I think I did well this week:
_____
_____

Nutrition Check-In

The good and bad of my food this week:
_____
_____

Days that I drank 8 glasses of water:

[S] [M] [T] [W] [T] [F] [S]

GRATITUDE MOMENT

This week, I feel thankful for: _____
_____
_____
_____

WRITE *THANK YOU* **NOTES PROMPTLY.**

NEVER GIVE UP ON ANYONE. MIRACLES HAPPEN EVERY DAY.

DATE _____ / _____ / _____

GOALS FOR THE WEEK

☐ A fitness goal for the week is: _____
_____

☐ A general goal for the week is: _____
_____

MOTIVATION CENTRAL

This week, I feel inspired by: _____

After working out, I'm totally going to: _____
_____

HOW AM I DOING?

Emotional Check-In

All in all, this week was:
_____
_____

One thing I think I did well this week:
_____
_____

Nutrition Check-In

The good and bad of my food this week:
_____
_____

Days that I drank 8 glasses of water:

[S] [M] [T] [W] [T] [F] [S]

GRATITUDE MOMENT

This week, I feel thankful for: _____
_____
_____
_____

DON'T WASTE TIME LEARNING THE 'TRICKS OF THE TRADE'. INSTEAD, LEARN THE TRADE.

INVEST YOUR TIME IN SOMETHING THAT MATTERS.

DATE _____ / _____ / _____

GOALS FOR THE WEEK

☐ A fitness goal for the week is: _____
_____

☐ A general goal for the week is: _____
_____

MOTIVATION CENTRAL

This week, I feel inspired by: _____

After working out, I'm totally going to: _____
_____

HOW AM I DOING?

Emotional Check-In

All in all, this week was:
_____
_____

One thing I think I did well this week:
_____
_____

Nutrition Check-In

The good and bad of my food this week:
_____
_____

Days that I drank 8 glasses of water:

[S] [M] [T] [W] [T] [F] [S]

GRATITUDE MOMENT

This week, I feel thankful for: _____
_____
_____
_____

RECOGNIZE AND ADDRESS ANGER WHEN YOU EXPERIENCE IT.

SURPRISE LOVED ONES WITH LITTLE UNEXPECTED GIFTS.

DATE ____ / ____ / _____

GOALS FOR THE WEEK

☐ A fitness goal for the week is: _____
_____

☐ A general goal for the week is: _____
_____

MOTIVATION CENTRAL

This week, I feel inspired by: _____

After working out, I'm totally going to: _____
_____

HOW AM I DOING?

Emotional Check-In

All in all, this week was:
_____
_____

One thing I think I did well this week:
_____
_____

Nutrition Check-In

The good and bad of my food this week:
_____
_____

Days that I drank 8 glasses of water:

[S] [M] [T] [W] [T] [F] [S]

GRATITUDE MOMENT

This week, I feel thankful for: _____
_____
_____
_____

NEVER MENTION BEING ON A DIET.

BE WORRY FREE.

DATE _____ / _____ / _____

GOALS FOR THE WEEK

☐ A fitness goal for the week is: _____
_____

☐ A general goal for the week is: _____
_____

MOTIVATION CENTRAL

This week, I feel inspired by: _____

After working out, I'm totally going to: _____
_____

HOW AM I DOING?

Emotional Check-In

All in all, this week was:
_____
_____

One thing I think I did well this week:
_____
_____

Nutrition Check-In

The good and bad of my food this week:
_____
_____

Days that I drank 8 glasses of water:

[S] [M] [T] [W] [T] [F] [S]

GRATITUDE MOMENT

This week, I feel thankful for: _____
_____
_____
_____

BE CLEAR ABOUT WHAT YOU WANT AND A SEE THROUGH TO IT.

_____
_____
_____
_____
_____
_____
_____
_____
_____
_____

DO NOT FALL FOR THE SAME OLD TRICKS AGAIN.

_____
_____
_____
_____
_____
_____
_____
_____
_____
_____

DATE _____ / _____ / _____

GOALS FOR THE WEEK

☐ A fitness goal for the week is: _____
_____

☐ A general goal for the week is: _____
_____

MOTIVATION CENTRAL

This week, I feel inspired by: _____

After working out, I'm totally going to: _____
_____

HOW AM I DOING?

Emotional Check-In
All in all, this week was:
_____
_____

One thing I think I did well this week:
_____
_____

Nutrition Check-In
The good and bad of my food this week:
_____
_____

Days that I drank 8 glasses of water:

[S] [M] [T] [W] [T] [F] [S]

GRATITUDE MOMENT

This week, I feel thankful for: _____
_____
_____
_____

LIVE SO THAT WHEN PEOPLE THINK OF FAIRNESS, CARING, AND INTEGRITY, THEY THINK OF YOU.

DEMAND EXCELLENCE AND BE WILLING TO PAY FOR IT.

DATE _____ / _____ / _____

GOALS FOR THE WEEK

☐ A fitness goal for the week is: _____
_____

☐ A general goal for the week is: _____
_____

MOTIVATION CENTRAL

This week, I feel inspired by: _____

After working out, I'm totally going to: _____
_____

HOW AM I DOING?

Emotional Check-In

All in all, this week was:
_____
_____

One thing I think I did well this week:
_____
_____

Nutrition Check-In

The good and bad of my food this week:
_____
_____

Days that I drank 8 glasses of water:

[S] [M] [T] [W] [T] [F] [S]

GRATITUDE MOMENT

This week, I feel thankful for: _____
_____
_____
_____

THE AMARA WOMAN WELLNESS JOURNAL | 55

LEARN TO MAKE SOMETHING BEAUTIFUL WITH YOUR HANDS.

YOUR TONGUE IS A SWORD OF POWER. USE IT WISELY.

DATE _____ / _____ / _____

GOALS FOR THE WEEK

☐ A fitness goal for the week is: _____
_____

☐ A general goal for the week is: _____
_____

MOTIVATION CENTRAL

This week, I feel inspired by: _____

After working out, I'm totally going to: _____
_____

HOW AM I DOING?

Emotional Check-In	Nutrition Check-In
All in all, this week was:	The good and bad of my food this week:
_____	_____
_____	_____
One thing I think I did well this week:	Days that I drank 8 glasses of water:
_____	[S] [M] [T] [W] [T] [F] [S]

GRATITUDE MOMENT

This week, I feel thankful for: _____
_____
_____
_____

THE AMARA WOMAN WELLNESS JOURNAL | 59

PRACTICE THE ART OF SILENCE.

___

EXPRESS GRATITUDE.

___

DATE _____ / _____ / _____

GOALS FOR THE WEEK

☐ A fitness goal for the week is: _____
_____

☐ A general goal for the week is: _____
_____

MOTIVATION CENTRAL

This week, I feel inspired by: _____

After working out, I'm totally going to: _____
_____

HOW AM I DOING?

Emotional Check-In

All in all, this week was:
_____
_____

One thing I think I did well this week:
_____
_____

Nutrition Check-In

The good and bad of my food this week:
_____
_____

Days that I drank 8 glasses of water:

[S] [M] [T] [W] [T] [F] [S]

GRATITUDE MOMENT

This week, I feel thankful for: _____
_____
_____
_____

BE WILLING TO DO IT DIFFERENTLY.

___

STEP BY STEP, YOU ARE GETTING BETTER AND BETTER.

DATE ____ / ____ / _____

GOALS FOR THE WEEK

☐ A fitness goal for the week is: _____
_____

☐ A general goal for the week is: _____
_____

MOTIVATION CENTRAL

This week, I feel inspired by: _____

After working out, I'm totally going to: _____
_____

HOW AM I DOING?

Emotional Check-In

All in all, this week was:
_____
_____

One thing I think I did well this week:
_____

Nutrition Check-In

The good and bad of my food this week:
_____

Days that I drank 8 glasses of water:

[S] [M] [T] [W] [T] [F] [S]

GRATITUDE MOMENT

This week, I feel thankful for: _____
_____
_____
_____

THE AMARA WOMAN WELLNESS JOURNAL | 67

EXPECT AS MUCH AS YOU CAN BECAUSE YOU CAN.

IN BUSINESS AND IN PERSONAL RELATIONSHIPS,
THE MOST IMPORTANT THING IS TRUST.

DATE _____ / _____ / _____

GOALS FOR THE WEEK

☐ A fitness goal for the week is: _____
_____

☐ A general goal for the week is: _____
_____

MOTIVATION CENTRAL

This week, I feel inspired by: _____

After working out, I'm totally going to: _____
_____

HOW AM I DOING?

Emotional Check-In

All in all, this week was:
_____
_____

One thing I think I did well this week:
_____
_____

Nutrition Check-In

The good and bad of my food this week:
_____
_____

Days that I drank 8 glasses of water:

[S] [M] [T] [W] [T] [F] [S]

GRATITUDE MOMENT

This week, I feel thankful for: _____
_____
_____
_____

THE AMARA WOMAN WELLNESS JOURNAL | 71

DO IT BY ANY MEANS HONORABLE AND NECESSARY.

HELP YOUR FRIENDS WITH THE THINGS THAT YOU KNOW.

DATE ____ / ____ / _____

GOALS FOR THE WEEK

☐ A fitness goal for the week is: _____
_____

☐ A general goal for the week is: _____
_____

MOTIVATION CENTRAL

This week, I feel inspired by: _____

After working out, I'm totally going to: _____
_____

HOW AM I DOING?

Emotional Check-In

All in all, this week was:
_____
_____

One thing I think I did well this week:
_____
_____

Nutrition Check-In

The good and bad of my food this week:
_____
_____

Days that I drank 8 glasses of water:

[S] [M] [T] [W] [T] [F] [S]

GRATITUDE MOMENT

This week, I feel thankful for: _____
_____
_____
_____

LIFE HAS TWO RULES: #1: NEVER QUIT!
#2: ALWAYS REMEMBER RULE #1.

FORGET THE JONESES.

DATE ____ / ____ / _____

GOALS FOR THE WEEK

☐ A fitness goal for the week is: _____
_____

☐ A general goal for the week is: _____
_____

MOTIVATION CENTRAL

This week, I feel inspired by: _____

After working out, I'm totally going to: _____
_____

HOW AM I DOING?

Emotional Check-In
All in all, this week was:
_____
_____

One thing I think I did well this week:
_____
_____

Nutrition Check-In
The good and bad of my food this week:
_____
_____

Days that I drank 8 glasses of water:

[S] [M] [T] [W] [T] [F] [S]

GRATITUDE MOMENT

This week, I feel thankful for: _____
_____
_____
_____

MAKE IT A HABIT TO DO NICE THINGS FOR
PEOPLE WHO WILL NEVER FIND OUT.

___

THINK BIG THOUGHTS AND RELISH SMALL PLEASURES.

DATE _____ / _____ / _____

GOALS FOR THE WEEK

☐ A fitness goal for the week is: _____
_____

☐ A general goal for the week is: _____
_____

MOTIVATION CENTRAL

This week, I feel inspired by: _____

After working out, I'm totally going to: _____
_____

HOW AM I DOING?

Emotional Check-In

All in all, this week was:
_____
_____

One thing I think I did well this week:
_____
_____

Nutrition Check-In

The good and bad of my food this week:
_____
_____

Days that I drank 8 glasses of water:

S M T W T F S

GRATITUDE MOMENT

This week, I feel thankful for: _____
_____
_____
_____

THE AMARA WOMAN WELLNESS JOURNAL | 83

YOU ARE IN CHARGE OF YOUR WORDS AND DEEDS.

LISTEN TO WHAT IS SAID, NOT TO WHAT YOU HEAR.

DATE _____ / _____ / _____

GOALS FOR THE WEEK

☐ A fitness goal for the week is: _____
_____

☐ A general goal for the week is: _____
_____

MOTIVATION CENTRAL

This week, I feel inspired by: _____

After working out, I'm totally going to: _____
_____

HOW AM I DOING?

Emotional Check-In

All in all, this week was:
_____
_____

One thing I think I did well this week:
_____
_____

Nutrition Check-In

The good and bad of my food this week:
_____
_____

Days that I drank 8 glasses of water:

[S] [M] [T] [W] [T] [F] [S]

GRATITUDE MOMENT

This week, I feel thankful for: _____
_____
_____
_____

THE HARVEST YOU REAP IS MEASURED BY
THE ATTITUDE YOU CULTIVATE.

REMAIN FOCUSED ON THE GOAL, EVEN IN THE MIDST OF BATTLE.

DATE _____ / _____ / _____

GOALS FOR THE WEEK

☐ A fitness goal for the week is: _____
_____

☐ A general goal for the week is: _____
_____

MOTIVATION CENTRAL

This week, I feel inspired by: _____

After working out, I'm totally going to: _____
_____

HOW AM I DOING?

Emotional Check-In

All in all, this week was:
_____
_____

One thing I think I did well this week:
_____
_____

Nutrition Check-In

The good and bad of my food this week:
_____
_____

Days that I drank 8 glasses of water:

[S] [M] [T] [W] [T] [F] [S]

GRATITUDE MOMENT

This week, I feel thankful for: _____
_____
_____
_____

YOU ARE A VALUABLE TOOL IN SOMEONE'S HEALING PROCESS.

BLESS SOMEONE ELSE TODAY.

DATE ____ / ____ / _____

GOALS FOR THE WEEK

☐ A fitness goal for the week is: _____
_____

☐ A general goal for the week is: _____
_____

MOTIVATION CENTRAL

This week, I feel inspired by: _____

After working out, I'm totally going to: _____
_____

HOW AM I DOING?

Emotional Check-In

All in all, this week was:
_____
_____

One thing I think I did well this week:
_____
_____

Nutrition Check-In

The good and bad of my food this week:
_____
_____

Days that I drank 8 glasses of water:

[S] [M] [T] [W] [T] [F] [S]

GRATITUDE MOMENT

This week, I feel thankful for: _____
_____
_____
_____
_____

LEARN TO LISTEN. OPPORTUNITIES SOMETIMES KNOCK VERY SOFTLY.

EXPLORING THE QUESTION BRINGS MORE
WISDOM THAN HAVING THE ANSWER.

DATE _____ / _____ / _____

GOALS FOR THE WEEK

☐ A fitness goal for the week is: _____
_____

☐ A general goal for the week is: _____
_____

MOTIVATION CENTRAL

This week, I feel inspired by: _____

After working out, I'm totally going to: _____
_____

HOW AM I DOING?

Emotional Check-In

All in all, this week was:
_____
_____

One thing I think I did well this week:
_____
_____

Nutrition Check-In

The good and bad of my food this week:
_____
_____

Days that I drank 8 glasses of water:

[S] [M] [T] [W] [T] [F] [S]

GRATITUDE MOMENT

This week, I feel thankful for: _____
_____
_____
_____

WHEN PLAYING GAMES WITH CHILDREN LET THEM WIN—SOMETIMES.

DO NOT ATTACK THE PROBLEM, GO THROUGH THE SOLUTION PROCESS.

DATE ____ / ____ / _____

GOALS FOR THE WEEK

☐ A fitness goal for the week is: _____
_____

☐ A general goal for the week is: _____
_____

MOTIVATION CENTRAL

This week, I feel inspired by: _____

After working out, I'm totally going to: _____
_____

HOW AM I DOING?

Emotional Check-In

All in all, this week was:
_____
_____

One thing I think I did well this week:
_____
_____

Nutrition Check-In

The good and bad of my food this week:
_____
_____

Days that I drank 8 glasses of water:

☐S ☐M ☐T ☐W ☐T ☐F ☐S

GRATITUDE MOMENT

This week, I feel thankful for: _____
_____
_____
_____

THE AMARA WOMAN WELLNESS JOURNAL

LOVE YOURSELF.

STRIVE FOR EXCELLENCE, NOT PERFECTION.

DATE ____ / ____ / _____

GOALS FOR THE WEEK

☐ A fitness goal for the week is: _____
_____

☐ A general goal for the week is: _____
_____

MOTIVATION CENTRAL

This week, I feel inspired by: _____

After working out, I'm totally going to: _____
_____

HOW AM I DOING?

Emotional Check-In

All in all, this week was:
_____
_____

One thing I think I did well this week:
_____
_____

Nutrition Check-In

The good and bad of my food this week:
_____
_____

Days that I drank 8 glasses of water:

[S] [M] [T] [W] [T] [F] [S]

GRATITUDE MOMENT

This week, I feel thankful for: _____
_____
_____
_____

FORGIVE AND YOU WILL BE FORGIVEN.

DON'T LOOK BACK.

DATE _____ / _____ / _____

GOALS FOR THE WEEK

☐ A fitness goal for the week is: _____
_____

☐ A general goal for the week is: _____
_____

MOTIVATION CENTRAL

This week, I feel inspired by: _____

After working out, I'm totally going to: _____
_____

HOW AM I DOING?

Emotional Check-In

All in all, this week was:
_____
_____

One thing I think I did well this week:
_____

Nutrition Check-In

The good and bad of my food this week:
_____
_____

Days that I drank 8 glasses of water:

[S] [M] [T] [W] [T] [F] [S]

GRATITUDE MOMENT

This week, I feel thankful for: _____
_____
_____
_____
_____

PRAY NOT FOR THINGS, BUT FOR WISDOM AND COURAGE.

BE TOUGH-MINDED YET TENDERHEARTED.

DATE ____ / ____ / _____

GOALS FOR THE WEEK

☐ A fitness goal for the week is: _____
_____

☐ A general goal for the week is: _____
_____

MOTIVATION CENTRAL

This week, I feel inspired by: _____

After working out, I'm totally going to: _____
_____

HOW AM I DOING?

Emotional Check-In

All in all, this week was:
_____
_____

One thing I think I did well this week:
_____
_____

Nutrition Check-In

The good and bad of my food this week:
_____
_____

Days that I drank 8 glasses of water:

[S] [M] [T] [W] [T] [F] [S]

GRATITUDE MOMENT

This week, I feel thankful for: _____
_____
_____
_____

DON'T WASTE TIME RESPONDING TO YOUR CRITICS.

_____

FOR EVERYTHING, THERE IS A SEASON.

_____

DATE ____ / ____ / _____

GOALS FOR THE WEEK

☐ A fitness goal for the week is: _____
_____

☐ A general goal for the week is: _____
_____

MOTIVATION CENTRAL

This week, I feel inspired by: _____

After working out, I'm totally going to: _____
_____

HOW AM I DOING?

Emotional Check-In

All in all, this week was:
_____
_____

One thing I think I did well this week:
_____

Nutrition Check-In

The good and bad of my food this week:
_____
_____

Days that I drank 8 glasses of water:

[S] [M] [T] [W] [T] [F] [S]

GRATITUDE MOMENT

This week, I feel thankful for: _____
_____
_____
_____

EVERY EXPERIENCE IS AN OPPORTUNITY TO GROW.

BE WILLING TO GIVE EVERYONE A FRESH START.

DATE _____ / _____ / _____

GOALS FOR THE WEEK

☐ A fitness goal for the week is: _____
_____

☐ A general goal for the week is: _____
_____

MOTIVATION CENTRAL

This week, I feel inspired by: _____

After working out, I'm totally going to: _____
_____

HOW AM I DOING?

Emotional Check-In

All in all, this week was:
_____
_____

One thing I think I did well this week:
_____
_____

Nutrition Check-In

The good and bad of my food this week:
_____
_____

Days that I drank 8 glasses of water:

[S] [M] [T] [W] [T] [F] [S]

GRATITUDE MOMENT

This week, I feel thankful for: _____
_____
_____
_____

YOU CAN DO ANYTHING YOU CHOOSE TO DO.

RESIST TELLING PEOPLE HOW SOMETHING SHOULD BE DONE. INSTEAD TELL THEM *WHAT* NEEDS TO BE DONE. THEY WILL OFTEN SURPRISE YOU WITH CREATIVE SOLUTIONS.

DATE ____ / ____ / _____

GOALS FOR THE WEEK

☐ A fitness goal for the week is: _____
_____

☐ A general goal for the week is: _____
_____

MOTIVATION CENTRAL

This week, I feel inspired by: _____

After working out, I'm totally going to: _____
_____

HOW AM I DOING?

Emotional Check-In

All in all, this week was:
_____
_____

One thing I think I did well this week:
_____
_____

Nutrition Check-In

The good and bad of my food this week:
_____
_____

Days that I drank 8 glasses of water:

[S] [M] [T] [W] [T] [F] [S]

GRATITUDE MOMENT

This week, I feel thankful for: _____
_____
_____
_____

THE AMARA WOMAN WELLNESS JOURNAL

BE ORIGINAL.

ONLY DO THOSE THINGS THAT FEEL RIGHT FOR YOU.

DATE ____ / ____ / _____

GOALS FOR THE WEEK

☐ A fitness goal for the week is: _____
_____

☐ A general goal for the week is: _____
_____

MOTIVATION CENTRAL

This week, I feel inspired by: _____

After working out, I'm totally going to: _____
_____

HOW AM I DOING?

Emotional Check-In

All in all, this week was:
_____
_____

One thing I think I did well this week:
_____
_____

Nutrition Check-In

The good and bad of my food this week:
_____
_____

Days that I drank 8 glasses of water:

[S] [M] [T] [W] [T] [F] [S]

GRATITUDE MOMENT

This week, I feel thankful for: _____
_____
_____
_____

YOUR INTENT WILL BE EVIDENT IN THE RESULTS.

___

___

___

___

___

___

___

___

___

BE KINDER THAN NECESSARY.

___

___

___

___

___

___

___

___

___

DATE ____/____/_____

GOALS FOR THE WEEK

☐ A fitness goal for the week is: _____
_____

☐ A general goal for the week is: _____
_____

MOTIVATION CENTRAL

This week, I feel inspired by: _____

After working out, I'm totally going to: _____
_____

HOW AM I DOING?

Emotional Check-In

All in all, this week was:
_____
_____

One thing I think I did well this week:
_____

Nutrition Check-In

The good and bad of my food this week:
_____
_____

Days that I drank 8 glasses of water:

[S] [M] [T] [W] [T] [F] [S]

GRATITUDE MOMENT

This week, I feel thankful for: _____
_____
_____
_____

BE ROMANTIC.

BE YOUR SIGNIFICANT OTHER'S BEST FRIEND.

DATE ____ / ____ / _____

GOALS FOR THE WEEK

☐ A fitness goal for the week is: _____
_____

☐ A general goal for the week is: _____
_____

MOTIVATION CENTRAL

This week, I feel inspired by: _____

After working out, I'm totally going to: _____
_____

HOW AM I DOING?

Emotional Check-In

All in all, this week was:
_____
_____

One thing I think I did well this week:
_____
_____

Nutrition Check-In

The good and bad of my food this week:
_____
_____

Days that I drank 8 glasses of water:

[S] [M] [T] [W] [T] [F] [S]

GRATITUDE MOMENT

This week, I feel thankful for: _____
_____
_____
_____

CHOOSE TO MARRY SOMEONE WHO YOU WOULD CHOOSE AS A FRIEND FIRST.

BECOME THE MOST POSITIVE AND ENTHUSIASTIC PERSON YOU KNOW.

DATE _____ / _____ / _____

GOALS FOR THE WEEK

☐ A fitness goal for the week is: _____
_____

☐ A general goal for the week is: _____
_____

MOTIVATION CENTRAL

This week, I feel inspired by: _____

After working out, I'm totally going to: _____
_____

HOW AM I DOING?

Emotional Check-In

All in all, this week was:
_____
_____

One thing I think I did well this week:
_____
_____

Nutrition Check-In

The good and bad of my food this week:
_____
_____

Days that I drank 8 glasses of water:

[S] [M] [T] [W] [T] [F] [S]

GRATITUDE MOMENT

This week, I feel thankful for: _____
_____
_____
_____

HAVE GOOD POSTURE. ENTER A ROOM WITH PURPOSE AND CONFIDENCE.

DON'T CARRY A GRUDGE.

DATE _____ / _____ / _____

GOALS FOR THE WEEK

☐ A fitness goal for the week is: _____
_____

☐ A general goal for the week is: _____
_____

MOTIVATION CENTRAL

This week, I feel inspired by: _____

After working out, I'm totally going to: _____
_____

HOW AM I DOING?

Emotional Check-In

All in all, this week was:
_____
_____

One thing I think I did well this week:
_____
_____

Nutrition Check-In

The good and bad of my food this week:
_____
_____

Days that I drank 8 glasses of water:

[S] [M] [T] [W] [T] [F] [S]

GRATITUDE MOMENT

This week, I feel thankful for: _____
_____
_____
_____
_____

CHOOSE WORK THAT IS IN HARMONY WITH YOUR VALUES.

_____

_____

_____

_____

_____

_____

_____

_____

COMMIT YOURSELF TO CONSTANT SELF-IMPROVEMENT.

_____

_____

_____

_____

_____

_____

_____

_____

DATE ____ / ____ / _____

GOALS FOR THE WEEK

☐ A fitness goal for the week is: _____
_____

☐ A general goal for the week is: _____
_____

MOTIVATION CENTRAL

This week, I feel inspired by: _____

After working out, I'm totally going to: _____
_____

HOW AM I DOING?

Emotional Check-In

All in all, this week was:
_____
_____

One thing I think I did well this week:
_____
_____

Nutrition Check-In

The good and bad of my food this week:
_____
_____

Days that I drank 8 glasses of water:

[S] [M] [T] [W] [T] [F] [S]

GRATITUDE MOMENT

This week, I feel thankful for: _____
_____
_____
_____

DON'T ALLOW THE PHONE TO INTERRUPT IMPORTANT MOMENTS. IT'S THERE FOR *YOUR* CONVENIENCE, NOT THE CALLER'S.

DON'T WASTE TIME GRIEVING OVER PAST MISTAKES. LEARN FROM THEM AND MOVE ON.

DATE _____ / _____ / _____

GOALS FOR THE WEEK

☐ A fitness goal for the week is: _____
_____

☐ A general goal for the week is: _____
_____

MOTIVATION CENTRAL

This week, I feel inspired by: _____

After working out, I'm totally going to: _____
_____

HOW AM I DOING?

Emotional Check-In

All in all, this week was:
_____
_____

One thing I think I did well this week:
_____
_____

Nutrition Check-In

The good and bad of my food this week:
_____
_____

Days that I drank 8 glasses of water:

[S] [M] [T] [W] [T] [F] [S]

GRATITUDE MOMENT

This week, I feel thankful for: _____
_____
_____
_____
_____

THE AMARA WOMAN WELLNESS JOURNAL | 155

THERE IS NO REASON TO SETTLE FOR LESS.

LOVING SOMEONE AND PLEASING SOMEONE ARE TWO DIFFERENT THINGS.

DATE ____ / ____ / _____

GOALS FOR THE WEEK

☐ A fitness goal for the week is: _____
_____

☐ A general goal for the week is: _____
_____

MOTIVATION CENTRAL

This week, I feel inspired by: _____

After working out, I'm totally going to: _____
_____

HOW AM I DOING?

Emotional Check-In

All in all, this week was:
_____
_____

One thing I think I did well this week:
_____
_____

Nutrition Check-In

The good and bad of my food this week:
_____
_____

Days that I drank 8 glasses of water:

[S] [M] [T] [W] [T] [F] [S]

GRATITUDE MOMENT

This week, I feel thankful for: _____
_____
_____
_____

THE AMARA WOMAN WELLNESS JOURNAL

SPEND LESS TIME WORRYING *WHO'S* RIGHT, AND MORE TIME DECIDING *WHAT'S* RIGHT.

DON'T MAJOR IN MINOR THINGS.

DATE _____ / _____ / _____

GOALS FOR THE WEEK

☐ A fitness goal for the week is: _____
_____

☐ A general goal for the week is: _____
_____

MOTIVATION CENTRAL

This week, I feel inspired by: _____

After working out, I'm totally going to: _____
_____

HOW AM I DOING?

Emotional Check-In

All in all, this week was:
_____
_____

One thing I think I did well this week:
_____
_____

Nutrition Check-In

The good and bad of my food this week:
_____
_____

Days that I drank 8 glasses of water:

[S] [M] [T] [W] [T] [F] [S]

GRATITUDE MOMENT

This week, I feel thankful for: _____
_____
_____
_____

THE AMARA WOMAN WELLNESS JOURNAL | 163

PRAISE IN PUBLIC. CRITICIZE IN PRIVATE.

WHEN SOMEONE HUGS YOU, LET THEM BE THE FIRST TO LET GO.

DATE ____ / ____ / _____

GOALS FOR THE WEEK

☐ A fitness goal for the week is: _____
_____

☐ A general goal for the week is: _____
_____

MOTIVATION CENTRAL

This week, I feel inspired by: _____

After working out, I'm totally going to: _____
_____

HOW AM I DOING?

Emotional Check-In

All in all, this week was:
_____
_____

One thing I think I did well this week:
_____
_____

Nutrition Check-In

The good and bad of my food this week:
_____
_____

Days that I drank 8 glasses of water:

[S] [M] [T] [W] [T] [F] [S]

GRATITUDE MOMENT

This week, I feel thankful for: _____
_____
_____
_____
_____

KEEP YOUR PROMISES.

SEEK OUT THE GOOD IN PEOPLE.

DATE _____ / _____ / _____

GOALS FOR THE WEEK

☐ A fitness goal for the week is: _____
_____

☐ A general goal for the week is: _____
_____

MOTIVATION CENTRAL

This week, I feel inspired by: _____

After working out, I'm totally going to: _____
_____

HOW AM I DOING?

Emotional Check-In

All in all, this week was:
_____
_____

One thing I think I did well this week:
_____

Nutrition Check-In

The good and bad of my food this week:
_____
_____

Days that I drank 8 glasses of water:

[S] [M] [T] [W] [T] [F] [S]

GRATITUDE MOMENT

This week, I feel thankful for: _____
_____
_____
_____

SHOW YOUR FAMILY HOW MUCH YOU LOVE THEM WITH YOUR WORDS, WITH YOUR TOUCH, AND WITH YOUR THOUGHTFULNESS.

_____
_____
_____
_____
_____
_____
_____
_____
_____

LEAVE EVERYTHING A LITTLE BETTER THAN YOU FOUND IT.

_____
_____
_____
_____
_____
_____
_____
_____
_____

DATE _____ / _____ / _____

GOALS FOR THE WEEK

☐ A fitness goal for the week is: _____
_____

☐ A general goal for the week is: _____
_____

MOTIVATION CENTRAL

This week, I feel inspired by: _____

After working out, I'm totally going to: _____
_____

HOW AM I DOING?

Emotional Check-In

All in all, this week was:
_____
_____

One thing I think I did well this week:
_____
_____

Nutrition Check-In

The good and bad of my food this week:
_____
_____

Days that I drank 8 glasses of water:

[S] [M] [T] [W] [T] [F] [S]

GRATITUDE MOMENT

This week, I feel thankful for: _____
_____
_____
_____

THE AMARA WOMAN WELLNESS JOURNAL | 175

NEVER UNDERESTIMATE YOUR POWER TO CHANGE YOURSELF.
NEVER OVERESTIMATE YOUR POWER TO CHANGE OTHERS.

PRACTICE EMPATHY. TRY TO SEE THINGS FROM
OTHER PEOPLE'S POINT OF YOU.

DATE ____ / ____ / _____

GOALS FOR THE WEEK

☐ A fitness goal for the week is: _____
_____

☐ A general goal for the week is: _____
_____

MOTIVATION CENTRAL

This week, I feel inspired by: _____

After working out, I'm totally going to: _____
_____

HOW AM I DOING?

Emotional Check-In

All in all, this week was:
_____
_____

One thing I think I did well this week:
_____
_____

Nutrition Check-In

The good and bad of my food this week:
_____
_____

Days that I drank 8 glasses of water:

[S] [M] [T] [W] [T] [F] [S]

GRATITUDE MOMENT

This week, I feel thankful for: _____
_____
_____
_____

DON'T BURN BRIDGES. YOU'LL BE SURPRISED HOW MANY TIMES YOU HAVE TO CROSS THE SAME RIVER.

___

DON'T SPREAD YOURSELF TOO THIN. LEARN TO SAY *NO* POLITELY AND QUICKLY.

___

DATE _____ / _____ / _____

GOALS FOR THE WEEK

☐ A fitness goal for the week is: _____
_____

☐ A general goal for the week is: _____
_____

MOTIVATION CENTRAL

This week, I feel inspired by: _____

After working out, I'm totally going to: _____
_____

HOW AM I DOING?

Emotional Check-In

All in all, this week was:
_____
_____

One thing I think I did well this week:
_____
_____

Nutrition Check-In

The good and bad of my food this week:
_____
_____

Days that I drank 8 glasses of water:

[S] [M] [T] [W] [T] [F] [S]

GRATITUDE MOMENT

This week, I feel thankful for: _____
_____
_____
_____

ACCEPT PAIN AND DISAPPOINTMENT AS PART OF LIFE.

REMEMBER THAT A SUCCESSFUL RELATIONSHIP DEPENDS ON TWO THINGS: 1) FINDING THE RIGHT PERSON, AND 2) BEING THE RIGHT PERSON.

DATE _____ / _____ / _____

GOALS FOR THE WEEK

☐ A fitness goal for the week is: _____
_____

☐ A general goal for the week is: _____
_____

MOTIVATION CENTRAL

This week, I feel inspired by: _____

After working out, I'm totally going to: _____
_____

HOW AM I DOING?

Emotional Check-In

All in all, this week was:
_____
_____

One thing I think I did well this week:
_____
_____

Nutrition Check-In

The good and bad of my food this week:
_____
_____

Days that I drank 8 glasses of water:

[S] [M] [T] [W] [T] [F] [S]

GRATITUDE MOMENT

This week, I feel thankful for: _____
_____
_____
_____

THE AMARA WOMAN WELLNESS JOURNAL

MEASURE YOUR SUCCESS BY THE DEGREE THAT YOU ARE ENJOYING PEACE, HEALTH, AND LOVE.

NEVER UNDERESTIMATE THE POWER OF LOVE. NEVER UNDERESTIMATE THE POWER OF FORGIVENESS.

DATE _____ / _____ / _____

GOALS FOR THE WEEK

☐ A fitness goal for the week is: _____
_____

☐ A general goal for the week is: _____
_____

MOTIVATION CENTRAL

This week, I feel inspired by: _____

After working out, I'm totally going to: _____
_____

HOW AM I DOING?

Emotional Check-In

All in all, this week was:
_____
_____

One thing I think I did well this week:
_____
_____

Nutrition Check-In

The good and bad of my food this week:
_____
_____

Days that I drank 8 glasses of water:

[S] [M] [T] [W] [T] [F] [S]

GRATITUDE MOMENT

This week, I feel thankful for: _____
_____
_____
_____

LEARN TO DISAGREE WITHOUT BEING DISAGREEABLE.

REFRAIN FROM ENVY. IT'S THE SOURCE OF MUCH UNHAPPINESS.

DATE ____ / ____ / _____

GOALS FOR THE WEEK

☐ A fitness goal for the week is: _____
_____

☐ A general goal for the week is: _____
_____

MOTIVATION CENTRAL

This week, I feel inspired by: _____

After working out, I'm totally going to: _____
_____

HOW AM I DOING?

Emotional Check-In

All in all, this week was:
_____
_____

One thing I think I did well this week:
_____
_____

Nutrition Check-In

The good and bad of my food this week:
_____
_____

Days that I drank 8 glasses of water:

[S] [M] [T] [W] [T] [F] [S]

GRATITUDE MOMENT

This week, I feel thankful for: _____
_____
_____
_____

THE AMARA WOMAN WELLNESS JOURNAL | 195

BE COURTEOUS TO EVERYONE.

DON'T DELAY ACTING ON A GOOD IDEA. CHANCES ARE SOMEONE ELSE HAS JUST THOUGHT OF IT, TOO. SUCCESS COMES TO THE ONE WHO ACTS FIRST.

DATE _____ / _____ / _____

GOALS FOR THE WEEK

☐ A fitness goal for the week is: _____
_____

☐ A general goal for the week is: _____
_____

MOTIVATION CENTRAL

This week, I feel inspired by: _____

After working out, I'm totally going to: _____
_____

HOW AM I DOING?

Emotional Check-In

All in all, this week was:
_____
_____

One thing I think I did well this week:
_____
_____

Nutrition Check-In

The good and bad of my food this week:
_____
_____

Days that I drank 8 glasses of water:

[S] [M] [T] [W] [T] [F] [S]

GRATITUDE MOMENT

This week, I feel thankful for: _____
_____
_____
_____

THE AMARA WOMAN WELLNESS JOURNAL | 199

REMEMBER THAT WINNERS DO WHAT LOSERS WON'T DO.

LIVE YOUR LIFE SO THAT YOUR EPITAPH COULD READ, "NO REGRETS".

DATE _____ / _____ / _____

GOALS FOR THE WEEK

☐ A fitness goal for the week is: _____
_____

☐ A general goal for the week is: _____
_____

MOTIVATION CENTRAL

This week, I feel inspired by: _____

After working out, I'm totally going to: _____
_____

HOW AM I DOING?

Emotional Check-In

All in all, this week was:
_____
_____

One thing I think I did well this week:
_____
_____

Nutrition Check-In

The good and bad of my food this week:
_____
_____

Days that I drank 8 glasses of water:

[S] [M] [T] [W] [T] [F] [S]

GRATITUDE MOMENT

This week, I feel thankful for: _____
_____
_____
_____

THE AMARA WOMAN WELLNESS JOURNAL | 203

NEVER WALK OUT ON A QUARREL WITH YOUR MATE.

DON'T THINK A HIGHER PRICE ALWAYS MEANS HIGHER QUALITY.

DATE ____ / ____ / _____

GOALS FOR THE WEEK

☐ A fitness goal for the week is: _____
_____

☐ A general goal for the week is: _____
_____

MOTIVATION CENTRAL

This week, I feel inspired by: _____

After working out, I'm totally going to: _____
_____

HOW AM I DOING?

Emotional Check-In

All in all, this week was:
_____
_____

One thing I think I did well this week:
_____
_____

Nutrition Check-In

The good and bad of my food this week:
_____
_____

Days that I drank 8 glasses of water:

[S] [M] [T] [W] [T] [F] [S]

GRATITUDE MOMENT

This week, I feel thankful for: _____
_____
_____
_____

BE BOLD AND COURAGEOUS. WHEN YOU LOOK BACK ON YOUR LIFE, YOU'LL REGRET THE THINGS YOU DIDN'T DO MORE THAN THE ONES YOU DID.

_____

_____

_____

_____

_____

_____

_____

_____

_____

_____

NEVER WASTE AN OPPORTUNITY TO TELL SOMEONE YOU LOVE THEM.

_____

_____

_____

_____

_____

_____

_____

_____

_____

www.ingramcontent.com/pod-product-compliance
Lightning Source LLC
Chambersburg PA
CBHW082108280426
43673CB00075B/252